POWERFUL QUOTES

QUOTES THAT MAKE YOU THINK

DEEPAK GUPTA

Contents

Before You Read This Book

Powerful quotes book is the compilation of all the quotes written in the books of Deepak Gupta. For the last five years, he has written many quotes that change the lives of people every day. And now he's sharing the best quotes in a separate book. If you are reading this, he hopes you will jump the highest wall to achieve your goals. He would like to thank everyone for reading his books. He's overwhelmed with the warm mails and messages he receives on social networking websites every day. A special thanks to everyone from the core of his heart. Have a wonderful read ahead. Stay calm, healthy and never stop dreaming.

Much Love + Gratitude

Deepak Gupta.

CHAPTER ONE

POWERFUL QUOTES

The whole world is full of fools. People are playing little with their destiny and dying in this busy world.

**

Small winnings are the bait to get caught in small games. Be the part of big games, where the challenge is much smarter than you, which can bring out the best in you.

**

Doors are open to all, but very few are entering.

**

Problems and solutions both are at the same place and lie in our minds, then; why do humans take decades to understand ourselves.

**

The world is full of lessons, deeds, opportunities, learning, growth, development, interaction, and life lessons. It's already open to us and depends on us how we try to get into it.

**

Implement those thoughts and suggestions, which we always give to others for being best, and I bet you would not

find the best suggestions in the world.
**

Life is not the destination; death is the destination as life is a journey. It depends on us whether to enjoy the journey or not and think about what we can do or to think about what we can't do. It's a matter of our thoughts.
**

Clean environment is the best nurture environment to bring out the best world-class thoughts and to think incredible even in the brutal conditions; The only matter is that, we must ensure how much great can we perform even in the poorest deadliest conditions.
**

Remove the mess and reduce stress.
**

To achieve your tremendous honest goal, you should ensure the greatness of your mind, the productivity of your mind, the real zest of your mind, and you will find a great change in your life that will bring out the best people around you.
**

Creativity takes courage and following our dreams takes much powerful courage.
**

To judge people and creatures through their faces is always a curse on this earth. We judge quickly by seeing the faces. Why is a lion always a killer? Now a day, lions are caged in the zoo, while some fools and culprits are wandering on the road independently.
**

Only the Ripple knows how powerful the sea is.
**

Have you ever walked alone in the dark night, even in the woods? Perfectly no, because we have a mind set that nights are scary, and days are safe; but my dear friend, the stars only shine at night. Be a little crazy about your life. One day we will die, but how would you feel that your fear would never die?

**

Come out of your pre-existing mindset which always says success is difficult and failure is easy. There are so many who have cracked a nut but don't know how they cracked it? They crave failure to learn something new, and for them success is much difficult at the end.

**

Don't surround yourself with more sea water, but surround yourself with the beautiful water.

**

Whenever time flies, life flies with the blissful face.

**

People have their own beliefs and norms. Some believe in their own psychology, while some try to come out in the middle of the strange crowd to understand other people's psychology. Very few have the exceptional genius mind to accept the ideas of god.

**

There is a complicated relationship between the attributes and elements of nature, even tougher and complicated than the strongest woven veins of the hearts of love birds. Some people think, love is the most complicated feeling in the world, but for someone love is simple as that. Difference is just the way we look at ourselves and others. Things look messy, if mess is in the nexus of our minds. This idea was never anonymous to wander, to search for the real nexus in the universe and the elements of the pure God; but unknowingly we ignore the real zest of our immortal world.

**

Silence is the music of God.

**

The day we forget our fear will become the best day to achieve anything in our life.

**

If an eagle fears then he would never be able to fly high. The world's biggest fear lies where the world's biggest success is hidden.

**

To judge others simply based on failure or success rate is a curse. Trust yourself, find your wise friends, and decide whether to love strangers or not.

**

Whenever we try to do something great, people will come towards us and laugh at us. This is universal law. Don't listen to them and ignore, and this is the real attribute of a beautiful mind.

**

Do your best every time irrespective of what you will get, because the right people always get the right people at the right time to do the right things. Right!

**

A crazy average mind is the real genius mind.

**

An average mind can do better than a genius mind until the average mind is much crazy than others.

**

Stitch your heart and open your mind, that's the only attribute I want people to remember.

**

Small is the beginning. Getting bigger is our own choice.
**

No one taught us that there was something beyond than the formal education. We are innocent and accept everything. They say, and we do.
**

If you don't give the right direction to your powers, you would end your life thinking that others have more power than you.
**

There's a big difference between being busy and being productive.
**

Silence has consistency, but words don't have it.
**

Chase the genius, he will tell us what turns us to become big.
Chase the fool, he will tell us, how much we are weak at understanding small things in life.
**

Successful people stories don't always work for us because they reveal what they experienced in their life on the basis of their own capability. Everyone has his own capabilities. Not everyone can swim when a tsunami comes.
**

If everyone agrees with your theory,
You are ordinary.
If some people agree with your theory,
You are innovative.
If no one agrees with your theory,
You are either a fool or an extraordinary,
but only time will tell your title.

**

Leaves shed
But the tree still grows.

**

I never wonder when I see people who failed in their school life, achieving the goals which were never achieved by those who were much intelligent in their school life. That's the lesson people teach us. Maybe you were not extra in your class but could have been extraordinary in your life.

**

Run away from ourselves, leaving us only at the initial point where we had started.

**

Money changes us even when we don't want to. That's the weakness we hold.

**

A clever tells a story while a wise lives it.

**

Don't treat human like God. God is perfect. We are human and we make mistakes.

**

Successful people have nothing except a wise and crazy mind.

**

Start takes courage and we blame fear every time.

**

The craziest people are wise personality,
But before they called wise, they were crazy.

**

Everyone should write once in his life and teach us what they think about the world, God and fantasies.

**

Your sun will rise when your sky appears blue.

**

Not every time God closes the door,
Sometimes we close our eyes deliberately.

**

A businessperson is much busy and much free personality in the world.

**

The man who loses before playing the game is neither a player nor a loser.

**

I have my own fear, but that fear never scares me enough to move forward.

**

Once someone asked what level of dedication a person should have?
You would still dedicate towards your goal even when the world's top 100 beautiful girls pass by you; I answered.

**

Before you live, feel the power inside. There are so many who are still sleeping.

**

When lazy becomes crazy,
Something drastic or amazing happens.

**

It takes the genius mind to teach and understand the dumb mind, and it takes the dumb mind to become the genius mind.

**

We don't have Plan A or Plan B. We have plans 1,2,3 and so on. Success is not defined by age. It's defined by determination.

**

A failure knows much better than a person who never fails.

Who has more plans?

A failure who is craving for success, or a successful person who never craved for failure.

**

Don't lose before you start; you will starve to become successful after lose.

**

Once I cried when I had no money, then I met a man who had much money but no life.

**

Being best is not the matter of achieving success again and again; instead it's about being passionate and crazy about the work even after getting failed.

**

Regret now to play small with your life, so that you can die peacefully with satisfaction and an inspiring success story, not with regrets and dreams.

**

Yes, there's a superhuman brain that lies or is hidden in the universe of our minds, but not everyone is using it because we don't even know whether it exists or not.

**

Don't play with time, otherwise the time has so many games to play with you.

**

Bring mental revolution into your life and your life will revolve.

**

Life is simple, yet complicated for different people.

**

God has just held your hand; you are writing your destiny and story.

**

Work bad, fail, get up again. Work hard, failure get up again. Work weirdly, fail, get up again. Work smartly, fail, get up again. Work passionately, fail, get up again. Work madly, success. Cheers. You don't need to get up; you did it already. Success is simply a recurring process of failure. To get through it is the only way. Failure is beautiful.

**

Your success story clap should be too loud, which lures others to do the same.

**

Life is a one-time opportunity. Do something great, otherwise the die is certain.

**

Success rate in your life depends upon your failure rate.

**

There's nothing like destiny in this world. It's just people's psychology to make themselves satisfied.

**

Resources are great, if you use it wisely. If you don't, then you are not wise.

**

The biggest challenge in our life is to challenge ourselves.

**

The whole world is full of baits. Don't baffle it with money only.

**

The real sailors always wait for the blizzard to show off their tremendous icy skills.

**

There's no need to conceal your benevolence; the world needs it the most.

**

Everything is mortal in this world except humanity and God. Both have the power to change the lives of others. Both have the power to change the perspective of this dynamic world. We need to bring both together to achieve the real aim in our life and we would become immortal persons in this mortal world.

**

It's better to be a failure than to be a second. As failure gives us the experience and lessons, but second only gives us the embarrassment to become first.

**

We should take risks in our lives, and those who don't, take risks in their whole lives.

**

You can't make your life easy, and if you make it then it's not life.

**

To feel tired with our goals is the first stage of our failure.

**

Enjoyment with our goal is the happiest moment in our life.

**

There's always a big opposition when we try to so something great in our life.

**

Nothing in this world is age restricted. You can think like a senior head on a young shoulder.

**

Now a day people are doing their passion as a hobby. We have a whole life to convert our hobby into passion and passion into opportunity.

**

If you can't trust yourself, then how can you expect it from others?

**

Being successful without lessons is not the good trademark of success.

**

Trees shed the leaves every day, doesn't mean it would completely shatter one day.

**

We are like buzzy bees flying everywhere to collect nectar but never tasted how sweet the honey is.

**

We don't have to chase the best things in life as it comes to us when we choose the right path with the right art.

**

Keep that in your mind, being busy is not always productive and being productive will never keep you busy in that.

**

Remember, if you want to lift the sky, your feet should be on the ground.

**

We all have different destinations according to our respective journeys, but people design us like everyone is the same. How do different people with different brains have the same goals? Looking weird, but somehow, we don't know who we are. We were born and accepted things like they were.

**

Formal education is necessary till we understand everything, and real-life education is much significant than any other education in the world.

**

There's vision in the eyes of people and art in hands. *I don't think making the portrait of someone is ordinary art. Can you do that?*

**

We all have some talent, but we are lost in making the things which never want to come around us.

**

The attributes which belong to us pull us always like food does for us when we are hungry. We don't have to push attributes.

**

We all have the fire to do something in our life, but forget that, flames would spread when the wind blows swiftly.

**

When we do nothing, we do everything - The Power of Nothing.

**

We will never get tired of doing the work we love and in the end; we find nothing and end up doing everything.

**

You are still fresh and enjoyable if you do the art you love and it would like nothing even when you are at the age of 99 and that's how successful people are always hungry and work for the art they love.

**

It's the matter of time and smart work which proves what we will grow whether the busy schedule or the productive environment.

**

If we do something with our heart, we can shake the mountain. Some see pebbles as mountains, while some see the mountains as pebbles. It's faith which brings success.

**

Be wise to accept everything like a child and rigid for honest art like a stubborn child.

**

Everything looks like nonsense when we start, but when people love nonsense it becomes good sense.

**

The world is so big, not everyone can stare at you.

**

You have to choose whether you want to hide your art in your heart or bring it out at the right time. If you keep it inside, it will break your heart, and if you bring it out, it will heal hearts.

**

Earning money is not the big task. Earning money while enjoying life is the big task.

**

People earn money through stress and spend it on entertainment. Okay that's not life.

**

We all are carved with beautiful art, but most of the people lose initially without knowing it. Unfortunately.

**

There's no risk until we start.

**

A day well lived is like cheating death for two more days.

**

If success was easy, then all would enter and make it crowded.

**

We all are lost in the spiral of thoughts, wanting to come up with the right thread.

**

We spend much time winning the life rather than understanding the life, and in between everything falls.

**

All persons are crazy and weird, but they would not reveal until you do. That's the mask in which we are real, may be weird, but the consistent, and real one we are searching for.

**

Don't go too far away, one day we have to look back to understand, what we have achieved and what we have lost during the journey of our life.

**

Not every mind is beautiful nor every heart resides the power of love.

**

There should be a perfect balance between our red heart and beautiful mind because sometimes we take decisions on the basis of our emotions and it really destroys us. And we know, not every person has a mind in his heart.

**

Time passes slowly for learners and fast for those who wait.

**

Being beautiful is the matter of a sacred soul, an immortal spirit, and a beautiful mind. Life is neither a race nor a destination. It's a beautiful journey with a beautiful mind.

**

Be courageous enough to walk alone as rare achievements are appreciated, not the ever-granted ones.
**

Cherish the Love in your heart, and grow the seed of your good deeds by watering it with the spirit of lessons.
**

Being successful without lessons is not the good trademark of success. We have to go down to understand the depth of success.
**

A successful person with the empty pot of failure is just the hollow success.
**

Great things happen when we perform great to prove ourselves, not to prove others.
**

The whole world is full of fools as they don't know about their capabilities. They are leaving their potential destiny and capabilities on the capabilities of others.
**

Beautiful things happen only once, wrong; beautiful things happen with the beautiful persons who know how to stare at the mirror and say, 'I can do it'.
**

There is a big gulf between survive and getting alive.
**

A survivor always gets more than his destiny because he loves his work, not the power of his destiny.
**

Because if we stopped on our way and threw pebbles at each other, we would end up destroying each other's mountains.
**

If the lion dances then the goat would surely come into the den.
**

At least love yourself before loving others.
**

Self inspiration is rare.
**

People don't run for money. They run for the comfort that money brings.
**

Believe in yourself or destiny. Both can't be on a team.
**

Time never comes if you wait.
**

Magic and coincidence look the same, but still much different. The former is the believer and the latter is the non-believer.
**

There's something greater than our problems, the way we respond to it.
**

The problem with our mind is that we focus on the thoughts which create problems in our mind, instead of finding out a thought which can help us to find a new perfect solution to our problems.
**

No one can respect you until you respect and love yourself.
**

There's a big gulf between education and values. Don't get confused between them.
**

Time and good deeds can do anything.

**

Most significant is how you react when people bring you down. That makes sense.

**

It's very easy to say wise words, but very difficult to follow it.

**

Readers and leaders both know how to imagine the whole world.

**

Defining others takes less time.
Define yourself,
It really takes much time.

**

Two types of mind are always happy,
One is a stable mind and the other is an empty mind.

**

Don't judge anyone too early.
Be late but accurate.

**

Don't live with double standards. Infact live with infinite inspiration.

About The Author

Deepak Gupta is pre-eminently known for writing plain sailing, meticulous, and pragmatic Self-Help books.

He's the author of **more than forty books** including **10 Principles to Beat Failure** that won **Google Best Choice 2018** & became **Top Seller on Google Play Store in 2019.** He has been garnering much acclaim for his **30 Minutes Read & 10 Principles Series.** Till now, he has received **490k+ readership & a lot of appreciation** from all over the world. He believes in writing & living best exceptional content from his subconscious mind. He loves to observe, absorb, and write on various social issues, inspirational truthful words, short stories, and heart whelming poetry. Also, he has travelled to many places in India like Manali, Rajasthan, Goa, Kolkata, Madhya Pradesh, Jammu, Dalhousie, and Mussoorie to bring descent originality in his work. He *releases new short books every month* to get readers to connect with the truth of life.

Deepak Gupta received his post-graduation degree from **Delhi School of Economics.** Also, when he's not writing, he can be found wandering on his **exquisite terrace garden.** He lives with his family in **Delhi, India.**

Keep in touch with Deepak via the web:
Instagram @authordeepakgupta
Facebook: facebook.com/authordeepakgupta
Twitter @authordeepakgup